LIVING WITH A PARENT
WHO TAKES DRUGS

Living with a Parent Who Takes drugs

Judith S. Seixas

GREENWILLOW BOOKS, New York

First Edition   10 9 8 7 6 5 4 3 2 1

Library of Congress Cataloging-in-Publication Data
Seixas, Judith S.
Living with a parent who takes drugs/Judith S. Seixas.
p.   cm.
Summary: case reports and explanatory text introduce the warning signs and
possible manifestations of drug abuse by a parent and ways of coping with such a problem.
ISBN 0-688-08627-6
1. Children of narcotic addicts—United States—Juvenile literature.
2. Narcotic addicts—United States—Family relationships—Juvenile literature.
3. Drug abuse—United States—Juvenile literature.
[1. Drug abuse.]   I. Title.
HU5824.C45S45   1989
362.2'92—dc19   89-1995   CIP   AC

In memory of my brother,
Herbert Carr Sartorius

Contents

LIVING WITH A PARENT
WHO TAKES DRUGS

Introduction

Many children live with one or both parents who take drugs. They wonder why their parents began using drugs and why they continue to use them when the drugs have become destructive to their families and harmful to their health.

The answers to these questions are not simple. And of course, the answers are different for different people. In the 1960s and 1970s drugs became popular, and it was not immediately known how harmful some of them could be and what damage they could do. Many people who were teenagers then began using drugs just for the fun of it, or in rebellion against their parents. Others were bored and found that drugs were a new and different experience. Our country was fighting a war in Vietnam, and some young people learned to ease the difficulty of dealing with a dangerous and what many believed was an unnecessary conflict by using drugs. For those who were in the armed forces drug use was also a kind of revolt against military regulations. Many, when they came back from the war, brought with them drug habits. One veteran said that when he went to war, he was drinking milk; when he came home, he was drinking whiskey.

During those years our "drug culture" grew. It included a special life-style, music, and clothing. Illegal drugs were part of that style. People found themselves victims of pressure from friends, or they simply gave in to fashion. They were expected to drink on special occasions; they were offered a variety of drugs on the street or at evening gatherings. Many found it difficult to say no. Others discovered drugs helped them relax or cope in stressful situations, such as breaking up with a longtime friend or mate, enduring illness, or losing a job. Some people began to take drugs to get them through the day or help them sleep at night. Others used prescribed drugs when they were sick and continued using them when they got well.

A few of the people who began to experiment with drugs or occasionally use them foresaw that someday they might not be able to stop. Others believed they could stop if they wanted to. But as it turned out, many people couldn't stop, and more people began buying, selling, and using drugs.

The drugs that were taken then and are still

most commonly used are alcohol and marijuana—one legal for people over twenty-one, the other illegal. Some people who began by drinking or smoking pot went on to use stronger mood-altering drugs. Like hairstyles, certain drugs become popular at different times. Trends change according to what drugs are around, how much they cost, and what friends are using. But dangerous drugs are always available for those who want them.

People who were in their teens and twenties in the sixties and seventies now have children. You may be one of those children. If so, this book is for you. Jason's story will help you understand your parent or parents. It will help you understand why some people continue to take drugs even when they know they are illegal and dangerous. You will read about how drugs complicate family ties. You will also find information about your rights, your responsibilities, and the law as it relates to drugs. This book will help you cope with pressures at home, in school, and from friends in your neighborhood. It will help you make thoughtful decisions about your own use of drugs, so you will want to avoid them.

1

A Family in Trouble

JASON

Jason was walking home from school. The load
of books in his backpack pulled on his shoulders
as he looked down at the cracks in the sidewalk.
He kept his eyes on the tree roots that grew
across the walk. When he spotted the twisted one,

he knew he was in front of his own house. His
mom would be at work, but he wondered if his
father would be there. He looked for a clue. He
walked through the alley to the back door and
peeked in the window. He could see the kitchen
table where his father might be sitting. From the
same spot he could see through the hallway to
the familiar living room. Perhaps his father
would be in his chair, looking at a silent TV. The
set would be on, but the volume would be off. The
radio would be blaring rock music. If Jason heard
the music, he would know his father was home.
There were other clues, too: the heavy checked
jacket hanging on the hook next to the back door,
and the smell of marijuana coming through the
cracks.

As he peered in, he saw his father lumbering
through the hallway. Jason's mind raced: Should I
go in? Did he see me? He's stoned and there will be
a hassle. I won't go in; I'll wait until later. It'll be
safer when Mom's home.

He dropped his books on the step and began
walking back toward school along the same way he
had come three minutes earlier. He felt lonely,
angry, worried, but, most of all, hungry. He hadn't

had anything to eat since he had devoured a skimpy bag of potato chips for lunch. Several boys from school came walking along.

"Jason, you're going the wrong way. School's over, man!" they teased.

"My aunt's waiting for me to come help with her chores," he called back. "I gotta hurry." And he rushed off toward the familiar green-shuttered house on the other side of the street where his father's sister lived.

His Aunt Grace opened the door and welcomed Jason with a big hug. Jason cringed, even though it felt good. Supposing his friends saw her putting her arms around him. They'd make fun of him the next day.

When would his aunt ask him if he wanted something to eat? First the endless questions about school: Did you play basketball? Was seventh-grade math still tough? Was his brother, Ronny, back in school after the flu? But the answers were hardly out of his mouth before she popped the next question. Why didn't she ask him about what was going on at home? She certainly knew something was wrong, but she would never talk about her brother. She acted as if he didn't exist, and her questions seemed pointless to Jason. At last she led him toward the kitchen, where he sat down to a peanut butter and jelly sandwich. He gulped a glass of milk to keep his tongue from sticking to the roof of his mouth.

Jason wanted more than anything to talk about the trouble at home, about his father, who smoked pot all day and paid no attention to the family. But he had been told, very firmly, not to mention to anyone what was going on, not to anyone at school, not to his friends, not to his neighbors, and particularly not to anyone in the family.

One day on the ball field Jason had heard his father called a pothead by one of his older brother's friends. He didn't want to hear the name-calling. He had put his hands over his ears. The sweet smell of marijuana had been around the house as long as he could remember. He wondered why his dad kept smoking pot when he and everyone in the house kept begging him to stop. His parents argued about it continuously. His mom was always in a bad mood. It was only recently that he realized that his father's smoking was the cause of so much trouble. But it seemed that the more his parents fought, the more his dad smoked.

A Family in Trouble

Jason didn't say a word. He had to face the fact that he couldn't talk to his aunt about his parents, but he couldn't stop his thoughts. I know I can't make it come true, but I sometimes wish my mom would marry another man. If only there had been a mistake and my Aunt Grace would turn out to be my real mother. Maybe I could just move in with her. She has room here for me. She's all alone. She might really need me. I could keep going to Hillside School. I could visit Dad and Mom even if they're not my real parents. I feel good here at Aunt Grace's. What would happen if I just stayed? Jason had to put these thoughts out of his mind.

But if he couldn't talk to his aunt, then whom could he talk to? His problems were not new, but recently everything seemed to disturb him more. He felt sadder. He found it difficult to pay attention in school even when he tried. He was having more and more headaches. He needed to talk to someone who would not just keep asking trivial questions. He wanted to know why his dad smoked marijuana the way kids did, why he felt so lonely, so unable to have fun with friends, so left out, so uneasy, so angry, so frightened. These feelings were getting worse.

He realized he needed help. He decided to talk to Mrs. Housemore, the student assistance counselor in school, who he knew was sworn to secrecy. He had never heard her talk about a student, and he knew she knew just about everything that went on at school. So the next morning he went directly to the student assistance office and asked for an appointment to see her.

"Come in, Jason," said Mrs. Housemore. "What's on your mind?"

"Well, things aren't going so well," said Jason. He was cautious. Maybe he shouldn't be here, after all. He'd been told not to talk about home at school.

"What's happening?" said Mrs. Housemore as she pulled her chair from behind her desk and sat closer to Jason.

"Well, I don't know. Well, you know . . . we had this thing about alcohol and drugs, and like I thought it would be a total drag, so I sat in back of the room. But I guess I knew what he was talking about."

"What do you mean?"

"I guess I'm sort of an expert," said Jason.

"Really?"

"My dad's got the problem." Jason lowered his

head, stared at the floor, but decided to continue. "Like he's doing pot all day. My mom's not home, she's at work, and he's sitting there smoking like a chimney . . . looks real spacy. When she gets home, there's always a fight. He hasn't cleaned up. He's left butts all over, and there's nothing ready for supper. She's tired. She goes for her cigarettes and swallows a pill or two, and then they start in. I get out of the way, and so does Ronny, but Dad punched him a couple of times—he's my older brother, remember him? He's a junior now; he's on the track team."

"Yes, I've seen him do the high jumps. Do you and Ronny talk about your parents?"

"Nah," said Jason, remembering the one time he brought up the subject and how Ronny had told him he was crazy, it was all in his head, and he should shut up.

"I want my dad to stop . . . I want him to be like other dads. . . . I hate our house. I hate everyone. I don't even like my best friends."

"It must be very scary for you," said Mrs. Housemore.

"Yeah. What if they catch him? What if he goes to jail?"

Jason was surprised that Mrs. Housemore was really listening. As he continued, he found he could talk more easily. Among other things, he told her about how often his father had promised that if he, Jason, would take out the garbage, he wouldn't smoke as much marijuana. But Jason didn't believe him anymore. Mrs. Housemore seemed to understand.

"There are three things I'd like you to remember and think about when you leave my office, Jason," she said. "One is that it's not your fault, no matter what you hear about why your father is smoking marijuana. You are not *causing* the drug use. Also, you can't *control* him and you can't *cure* him. Remember those three *C*s. Also, I'd like to see you again soon. Can you come back at the end of the week?"

Jason nodded and walked slowly out of her office. "See you later," he said.

He thought Mrs. Housemore might really be able to help him, and he trusted her. He just wanted to be less confused and more able to concentrate on his work at school, rather than worry all day about what his father was doing and then feel in a panic as the time to go home came closer.

A PARENT ON DRUGS

Many young people who live with parents who take drugs feel just as confused, embarrassed, and unhappy as Jason. Of course, they love their parents, but at the same time they feel betrayed. When they realize their families are different from others, they feel angry and they search for ways to cope. Some make up for their unhappiness by excelling in school or in sports. Often the oldest child in a family will become a family caretaker and see to it that things run smoothly when there is no parent there to take care of the household details, such as getting the meals, cleaning up, or seeing that the younger ones get dressed and off to school. And he or she helps them with their schoolwork and often guards them from harm when they are outside in the yard or street.

Other children cope by being very quiet and staying clear and away from what is going on at home. They hide in their rooms, they bury themselves in books, or they stay with friends if they can. They try not to be seen or heard around the house. On the other hand, there are some children who make a lot of noise, act silly, clown, or do cartwheels in the living room so the attention is on them and not on the parents who are stoned or drunk. Some children will take the blame for small accidents such as a broken glass or spilled milk in order to prevent a fight between their parents. The various things children do to cope usually work, at least for a while. But in the long run they cannot solve the drug problem.

Children who live with parents who are taking drugs often dream that life in a different place would be better. They think of places that would be safer. Such a place is not always, as it is for Jason, the home of a relative. It might be the home of a friend or a teacher, a camp counselor's home, or a neighbor's house. Many kids find a part-time solution. They spend time after school or on weekends at a youth center, a mall, a playground, or a library, or baby-sitting for a neighbor.

Jason's dreams and wishes are common ones. Perhaps you have had similar thoughts. If you, like Jason, are living with a parent who uses one or more drugs, probably you, too, have been hurt or disappointed. There is a good chance, too, that you are very angry. It is important to let that anger out. Then you won't take it out on friends or people you like and respect. There are various ways people use to express their anger: talking about it, exercising vigorously, yelling at the tops of their lungs (out of earshot, of course). You may want to look for a way that works for you.

It took a lot of courage for Jason to go to see the student assistance counselor, Mrs. Housemore, because he was revealing the family secret for the first time. But it turned out that he had taken a step that would lead to help for him and his family. It's always difficult to do something new or to take a chance on rocking an already unsteady boat. But if you feel at a loss or confused about what is happening in your home, you might think about taking the same brave step Jason took toward getting help.

2

Mrs. Housemore's List

JASON

The next time Jason walked into Mrs. Housemore's office he began by saying, "I'm not sure there's really a problem with my dad. Maybe I just think there's something wrong. . . . Maybe it's kind of all in my head."

Mrs. Housemore replied, "I have a questionnaire here that I give kids who aren't really sure whether or not anyone at home has a drinking or drug problem. There are only ten questions. Answer yes or no to each one. When you're finished, you'll know whether or not there's a problem. You don't have to tell me your answers. You'll know in your own mind."

Jason studied the list:

1. Have you ever wished that your mom or dad would use fewer drugs, would drink less, or would stop using drugs or alcohol?

2. Have you ever worried about your mom's or dad's health because of what drugs or medications were doing to him or her?

3. Have you ever been kept awake by your parents' arguments after they had gotten high or had too much to drink?

4. Have you ever worried about your parents' fights or arguments while they were using drugs or drinking?

5. Have you ever cried or felt sick as you worried about your mom's or dad's drug use or drinking?

6. Did you ever protect another family member from a parent who was drinking too much or using drugs?

7. Has a parent ever made you promises that were broken because of drinking or drug use?

8. Have you ever been blamed for your mom's or dad's drinking or use of drugs?

9. Have you ever wished your home were more like the homes of your friends who have parents who don't drink or use drugs, or overdo it on prescribed medications?

10. Have you ever thought of running away from home because of a parent's drinking or drug use?

Jason was dazed after he read the list. He had answered yes to every question except number six. He couldn't honestly recall a time when he had had to protect Ronny or his mother from his father, although he thought that the day might come when he would have to. Mrs. Housemore then spent some time talking with Jason and explaining how drugs such as marijuana can affect a parent, how that parent can affect the rest of the family, and some of the reasons why people use marijuana. She then began to help Jason figure out how he could better cope with his father's drug use. She asked, "What will you do when your father loses control and you don't know what will happen next?"

"Well, one thing I *won't* do is get in his way, but I can't always get out of the house. It's really rough on weekends. I stay in my room a lot. Sometimes I go to Ronny's room, but he gets really upset if I touch any of his stuff. Sometimes I go down to the basement and work on my bike there. If I hear Dad coming, I try to get by him and go upstairs. My mom's no help. She doesn't pay much attention to me, and she picks a fight with him even when he's stoned. When they say really mean things to each other, I slap my hands over my ears or listen to my Walkman. In bed I cover my head with my pillow."

"Jason, when things get that rough, you should plan for your own safety. If things get bad enough, you may have to leave the house and call for help. If you must get out, think ahead of a place where you can go. Be sure to let your mother know about your plans ahead of time. However, if you just need to be out of the house until your mom comes home, there are things you can do. Do you belong to any clubs? Have you tried the 'Y' or the community center?" She added, "I'll tell you what. I'll help you find the programs that meet after school. Then we'll get your mother's permission and you'll have a safe place to go."

"Great!" said Jason, staring at his feet. Again he felt relieved that at last someone was listening to him, taking him seriously, and offering ways to help him.

EVERYTHING IS NOT OKAY

If you answered yes to any of the questions Mrs. Housemore gave to Jason, at least one of your parents probably has a serious problem with drugs, or alcohol, or both. You don't have to wonder about your own ability to see the truth. You may wonder why you deny the truth. Perhaps it's because your parents tell you that everything is okay. You may want very much to believe them. And you may want to believe that everything in your home is normal. But it isn't.

Your parents may tell you that it's your fault when they drink or use drugs. Your mom or dad may try to convince you that if you were only different, things would be better. You may believe it, too. For example, you may think that if you did better in school, your mom wouldn't drink so much. Or if you helped in the kitchen without being asked, she wouldn't have to resort to pills. Or if you cleaned out the car on Saturdays, your dad wouldn't be so nervous and impatient. One thing to remember is that people who use drugs are looking for excuses. They blame their drug use on anything and anyone they can. You may have heard your dad blaming the weather or his boss or your mom blaming her outdated car. It may be that if you bring home a bad grade, you give them an excuse to get angry. Then they will tell you that your poor school performance is the reason they take more of whatever drugs they are on.

No matter what, nothing you do or don't do will change their drug use. There may be some ways you can help yourself and your family, but you can't change your parents' behavior, because their problems have nothing at all to do with your behavior, good or bad. Remember you may do things that get your father angry, but only he can decide how to handle his anger.

TRY THINKING ABOUT YOU

Some young people live with drug-abusing parents who started using drugs all of a sudden because of some upsetting situation. They remember when their parents were different, and they wish that their parents would again be the way they were. Others have lived with drug-using parents for as many years as they can remember. Many may not be able to recall a time when their mother or father was not gulping drinks, downing pills, or using some kind of chemical. You may not be able to remember a drug-free day. Children need to think about doing things for themselves. There are simple everyday things that children can do to comfort themselves, at least temporarily. They can read a book, do homework, play games, or talk to a trustworthy friend on the phone. Or they might go for a bike ride or take a walk. They might earn some money by walking a neighbor's dog, or watering a neighbor's plants or garden, or helping elderly people with their shopping by carrying packages.

NOT ALL PARENTS ARE LIKE THIS

It is frightening to be living in the midst of what appears to be crazy behavior. Your dad may be loving one moment, and the next he may be in an awful mood and yell at everyone. You may think this is the way all dads are, but it really isn't. Most people have mood swings, just as you do. Sometimes you feel the world isn't fair. Other times you may feel more positive. But extreme behaviors, either highs or lows, are not normal.

It is the drug at work that makes tempers rise and fall. Think about almost any even-tempered adult you may know—the parent of a friend, a relative, or a teacher—and you will know that he usually can be counted on to mean what he says and to do what you expect of him.

After you have seen so much that is difficult to understand, you may wonder what it feels like to be under the influence of alcohol or drugs. Have you ever had a very high fever? Think how you felt then. Was it a fuzzy feeling, a feeling of being outside yourself and looking in from a distance? Or was everything much brighter and louder? Perhaps it was difficult to make your body react the way it usually does. This is how it feels to your parent when he or she is drinking or taking a drug. That person is out of touch with the real world.

Even when you understand why your parent is taking a drug or how he feels when he's had too much, don't be tempted to believe that nothing is wrong. This is not the way families should be. Most families count on one another to help and to be there when they are needed. So, when a parent is sick or not able to do his part, everyone is affected. Understanding may be a first step. But it is not enough. As time goes on, something must be done to change the situation.

WHO CARES?

It's not only fighting that upsets kids. What might be just as upsetting is a time when your mom or dad is not paying attention or doesn't seem to care. You may think this means that your parent doesn't love you. But remember, what your parent is doing with drugs has nothing to do with whether or not you are loved. When parents take drugs, it is often hard for them to show their love for their children, and drugs often make parents do things that make their children feel unloved.

Some children find that it is impossible to get their parents' attention even when they shout. One girl said she had to tug on her mother's skirt until it began to slip down before she could get her attention. When her mother didn't listen to her, she thought it meant her mother didn't love her. What made things worse was that the girl felt that she didn't deserve her mother's affection. She was sure that her mother's lack of caring was her fault; she was not a good enough child.

CONFUSION AND DENIAL

Children who live with parents who use drugs are often confused in addition to being frightened.

They have trouble knowing what is right and what is wrong, because their parents tell them one thing one day and something altogether different at another time. A parent may permit a child to stay up late one night, and the next night stick to a nine o'clock bedtime. Or a parent may say something like "Rules are made to be obeyed." And then the child may see that same parent drive knowingly through a red light. Without help it is difficult to sort out truth from lies. When you have been disappointed or given conflicting information for years, you will need to find someone to help you gain confidence in your own judgment.

Children may deny that there are any problems. This is often easier than admitting to the truth. They may not want to face the truth when they learn that people who take too many drugs are sick and that alcoholism is an illness. They've heard of drug "overdoses," and they worry when they know parents could die from too much of a drug. They may feel ashamed and not want anyone to know about the drug use, particularly when they eventually learn that their parents are doing something illegal. They have heard of "drug busts" and have learned what the consequences of illegal drug use can be.

ANDREA

One ten-year-old girl, Andrea, was told by both her parents that she would be "smacked good" if she told anyone in school about her father's drinking or her mother's pill taking. Many times she had seen her mother rushing for the pills. Even though they had been prescribed by the doctor and she had been told her mother took them for headaches, Andrea had an uneasy feeling. It grew even worse when she began to find hidden empty gin bottles in odd places around the house. The one that surprised her the most had been under the pillow in the dog's basket.

Finally she couldn't hold the secret in any longer. Her mother was "out of it" every night. No one fixed dinner, cleaned up, or took care of her seven-year-old brother and her little two-year-old sister. Andrea had to talk to someone. She decided to talk to a person outside school. Then she wouldn't really be disobeying her parents. There was a counselor in the community center who would understand. She told him about her father's drinking and her mother's pills. She asked for help for her sister, who was being neglected during the day. The counselor reported what Andrea had said to a child-care person who worked in a family agency. Andrea's grandmother was called.

When Andrea's brother heard that she had told the counselor about their family, he was surprised and really scared. He knew they were not supposed to talk to anyone. He thought he was the one who would be beaten because the girls usually got off more easily. However, their grandmother went to their house right away. Luckily, Andrea's mom didn't seem to mind when her own mother took over. She was feeling overwhelmed by her job, the children, and lack of sleep. The pills, which had helped at first, were now only making her jittery. And Andrea's dad didn't care what happened as long as the children kept out of his way. Andrea's grandmother continued to stay with them. She helped make meals, read to the children, and got them ready for bed. In the mornings she helped Andrea fill her lunch box and get off to school, and she took the baby to a day-care center. Most important, she protected all three children from their parents. If it hadn't been for Andrea's courage, things could have gotten much worse.

WHOM CAN YOU TALK TO?

Because children are often told by both parents that they will be punished if they talk to anyone at school about what goes on at home, many children distrust their teachers or school counselors. Sometimes they are even told not to talk to relatives. What happens inside your home is private business. But there are times when you must tell, particularly if keeping the secret makes you feel uncomfortable or unsafe.

If you don't know someone like Mrs. Housemore, whom can you talk to comfortably? Is there a youth counselor or a social worker at a youth center in your school or town? If you have been to family court or have been involved some way with the law, is there a probation officer you trust or a police youth officer? Or perhaps you can talk to your family's minister, priest, or rabbi and trust him or her to keep your secret? Do you have a relative in whom you can confide? Do you have an older sister, brother, or friend with whom you can share your worries? Keep your eyes out for the right person. The person you can trust right now is someone who:

Listens to you,

Responds to you in a way that makes you know she's heard what you've said,

Doesn't put you down, and takes you seriously,

Makes you feel you want to see him or talk to him again,

Can take some action if it is needed.

3

The Law

JASON

Jason was in Mrs. Housemore's office again.

"How are you, Jason?"

"Well, I've got a headache. . . . I was thinking maybe I'd go to the nurse's office and get excused. But then I thought I would rather come see you."

"Have you had headaches before?"

"Yes, it's just that they're getting worse. . . . I can't think straight. Funny I said that. . . . Nothing's straight; everything's a mess. Right now I can't find my leather jacket. . . . I think my dad sold it. . . . The toaster's gone, too. It doesn't matter, there's no bread. Whenever Dad needs cash, something goes. Do you know what our Christmas surprise was?"

"No, what?"

"He sold the TV. There was just a big blank space in the corner of the living room. But Dad couldn't do without it. The next day he got a tiny black-and-white one.

"Mom's kind of spacy, too. She got the doctor to give her a bunch of pills; they're called Valium. Anytime she calls him he prescribes thirty pills. He sure doesn't know what *she's* doing! Then she makes excuses for Dad, keeps telling us to stay out of his way like he's feeling bad this once. She yells at him, tries to get him to go look for work. He tells her to shut up. She does, and pops another pill and quiets down. And Ronny doesn't come home much anymore. He can't stand it around the house. Last year he got in trouble for cutting classes and not showing up at school. They threatened to take him to court in the PINS program (Persons in Need of Supervision), so he straightened out. He used to stick close to home and take care of things. Now he hangs out with his group of kooks."

"Jason," said Mrs. Housemore, "I can see you're pretty much on your own."

"I guess so."

Jason stopped talking. He began to worry. If any of this gets out, I'm sure to be grounded or worse, he thought. Again Mrs. Housemore tuned in on what Jason was thinking.

"I want you to know, Jason, that nothing you say to me will go farther than this room or go on any of your records. Only if you are really being abused or neglected, or if you are in danger of harming yourself or someone else, will I have to say anything to anyone."

The very next day Jason asked to see Mrs. Housemore again. When he arrived in her office, he looked pale, his eyes had blue shadows under them, and he dragged his feet.

"Jason, what's bothering you?" Mrs. Housemore asked. There was a long pause. "Come on, Jason. What happened?"

"Uh, there was a fight last night," he said. "My

dad got real high on something and hit my mom. Her head was bloody. She went to the hospital and had twelve stitches."

"That sounds pretty bad, Jason. Is she okay now?"

"Yeah. She went to work with a big bandage on her forehead."

"Jason, I think you should know more about what this could mean to you. You know your dad is doing something illegal and dangerous. The law does not suggest that children turn their parents in when they know they are breaking it. However, you should not have to hide what your parents are doing. You need help. And so does your father.

"Now it is up to me to put a call in to Child Protective Services so that you, too, don't get beaten up." Mrs. Housemore got up. "I'd like you to go back to class now. I'll check back with you after I've made some calls. While I'm working, you need to keep reminding yourself that you can't solve your parents' problems alone. However, when the fighting becomes dangerous, something has to be done to see that you and Ronny don't get hurt. Jason, this telephone call might make a big difference."

Jason was mixed up. He really didn't want Mrs.

Housemore talking to anyone about his family. At the same time he knew they needed help.

"I don't want any changes," he said. "Everything's really okay." But then he added, "I think I'm starting to hate my father. I mean, I just really hate him."

Jason was shivering. He put his head down on the desk in front of him. He thought he might cry. Mrs. Housemore tried to comfort him.

"Remember, you don't always have to feel good; you can accept these sad feelings and know that it's okay to feel this way when things are not going well."

MELANIE'S STORY

Melanie's mother was a cocaine addict. She was serving a three-month term in prison for shoplifting. She stole from department stores—jewelry, clothing, and small items which she could sneak off shelves and slip into her shopping bag. One time she walked out of a store in a brand-new pair of shoes. Another time she got away with a hair dryer. Most of the things she stole were items she could sell again quickly so she would have money to buy cocaine.

Melanie learned the value of designer clothes from her mother. She often amazed her classmates. "Hey," she'd say. "Look at that Calvin Klein blouse." The kids were really impressed. But Melanie knew when her mother told her she had forgotten to pay, she was only making an excuse. Melanie knew her mother was breaking the law.

Several weeks after Melanie's mother was arrested and imprisoned, Melanie's grandmother took her to the prison on a visiting day. Melanie was amazed to find her mother there, because at first her grandmother had told her that her mother was in the hospital. She said she'd had an accident and would be home soon. Melanie believed her grandmother, who had been ashamed to tell the girl the truth. Every day Melanie had waited for her mother to come home. Now, seeing her, she felt better. After a while they went outside and sat together on the fenced-in lawn.

Melanie didn't care where they were as long as she could hold her mother's hand and sit close, leaning against her. She told her mom all about school and about her teacher who never smiled.

During the visit Melanie's mother told her she would be coming home soon, and that she was not going to steal anymore. For the first time she was honest with Melanie. She told her she had been on cocaine, but was now off it. She would no longer need money to buy the drug. She also explained some other things that had been puzzling Melanie: why she had kept the shades down even in daytime and why she had talked in a hushed voice whenever they went shopping together. People on cocaine, she told Melanie, think they are being watched and listened to all the time.

Together Melanie and her mother made a calendar so Melanie could cross off the days until her mother would come home for good. Melanie taped it up on the wall above her bed. On the way home she said to her grandmother, "People who use drugs are bad, but my mom isn't. She just got in with some bad people."

Her grandmother nodded, but added, "They're not really bad. Those people are sick."

This story happens to have a happy ending. However, they don't all happen that way.

NEGLECT AND ABUSE

The age at which you are legally a minor ranges from sixteen to twenty-one, depending on which state you live in. A minor is NEGLECTED if parents or persons legally responsible for that child don't supply food, clothing, a home, education, and medical care if they have enough money to do so. Any child who is abandoned or left alone for long periods of time is also considered neglected. Parents must also take care of their children and protect them from harm. Another sign of a parent's neglect may be a minor who is using drugs or drinking.

A child is ABUSED when a parent or anyone who is responsible for the child's care allows physical harm to come to that child. That does not include accidents. A parent or other person responsible for the well-being of a child also must protect the child's mental or emotional health. If that is not being done, the child is abused. All children should have a safe place to live and a trusted person to talk to.

DRUGS AND SEX ABUSE

People who take drugs may lose control, lose their inhibitions, and ignore what is right and what is wrong. Sometimes they become involved in sex abuse. You must know that you have a right to be in charge of your own body. You don't have to do anything personal that doesn't seem right or feel right. Any sex offense against a child is considered abuse. That means when an older child or grown-up involves you in a sexual way, it is sex abuse. If an older child, a grown-up, or one of your parents touches your sex organs at all, that is sex abuse. If you are asked to kiss or touch the sex organs of a person older than yourself, that is sex abuse. If anyone hugs or kisses you in a way that is not just everyday affection, that is sex abuse. Even if it's your parents, if you are asked to play sex games or watch sexual acts, that is sex abuse. If you are forced to have sexual intercourse, that is sex abuse.

If you are sexually abused, it is not your fault. You are not to blame. But even if you are embarrassed, you must tell a responsible person what is happening. Then you will not be left alone with your feelings of guilt or feelings of having caused the abuse. You also will have less chance of catching a disease, such as AIDS, which can be spread by sexual contact.

When trusted adults know about the sex abuse, steps can be taken to prevent it from continuing. But those steps have to be taken by someone who has some power and authority. For your sake, or the sake of any young person, it should be stopped right away.

HOW THE LAW WORKS

The law is on the side of children. In most states it is a federal crime to sell drugs in schools or near school grounds. The law is also supposed to prevent maltreatment or abuse. And it is supposed to help parents protect themselves as well as their children. It is not meant to punish parents. The law assumes that the best way to help children is to help their families. Neglect and abuse are danger signs. They mean a family is in trouble and needs help.

The law is very clear about people who possess, use, or sell drugs. However, the law varies from state to state. In most states it is unlawful to give, sell, serve, or permit service of *alcoholic* beverages to anyone under age twenty-one. In most states adults are responsible for negligence when they have provided alcohol or drugs to minors. This means that an adult who gives alcohol or drugs to a minor can be held responsible for all damages to persons or property caused by a minor who is under the influence of alcohol or a drug. It is also unlawful for an adult to hold a party in his home at which minors are allowed to drink alcohol—except during religious ceremonies.

In most states it is unlawful to sell *tobacco* products to minors. And in some states the possession of small amounts of *marijuana* is not a crime. But in New York State a person who possesses up to two ounces of marijuana can go to jail for ninety days and/or be fined five hundred dollars. A person caught smoking it in public can go to jail for up to three months. The dealer or person who sells marijuana can go to prison for a year.

There are more severe punishments for possessing or selling *narcotics*. Penalties for carrying *crack* are also very severe. If you are caught with five vials (five hundred milligrams) of crack, you may go to prison for one to seven years. Selling it may bring the seller a sentence of up to twenty-five years in prison. Even a "gift" of some drugs may result in a sentence of life imprisonment. The punishment depends on what kind of drug is being carried, sold, or given away.

Parents and guardians who are responsible for the care of minors should know the consequences of breaking any of our laws. Parents should know the laws and how they work.

4

When Families Must Break Up

JASON

The next morning in second-period math class Jason could hardly keep his eyes on the blackboard. He couldn't concentrate long enough to understand a thing the teacher was talking about. At last toward the end of the hour a messenger came from Mrs. Housemore's office with a note asking that Jason be excused to come see her. He ran through the halls and down to her office in record time.

"Hi, Jason. I made the phone calls."

"What did they say?"

"I talked to the worker at Child Protective Services late yesterday. You don't need to worry. They're not in any rush to make changes. I have to file this report. Let me show it to you." And she showed Jason a blank form. All he could see were spaces that still needed to be filled in. One section he noticed was headed "Basis of Suspicions." He pointed to it.

"What does that mean?"

"'Basis of Suspicions' means they want to know why I think there is something going on in your family that isn't quite right. I will have to tell them about the fight between your mom and dad. If they think it's too dangerous at home, they may want your mom to sign a complaint. If she is willing to sign it, she will report your father to the police. This is known as pressing charges."

"She's not going to sign anything. She won't even sign my report card. . . . I have to get Dad to do it, and that's not easy."

"Well, if things get bad enough, your mom might agree to get an order of protection from the court. That would mean that your dad would be arrested if there's any more serious fighting. The possibility of an arrest might get him to go for help. Your mother could tell him that she won't bring charges or go to court at all if he agrees to go into a treatment program."

Jason shrugged his shoulders. "She'd never do any of that," he said.

"Well," said Mrs. Housemore, "if she won't, then there's a possibility that Child Protective Services will want you and Ronny to move out. They would find a safer place for you to stay until your dad decided to get some help. And it often happens that when a report is about to be sent in to CPS, parents get frightened and agree to make a change. If this happened, it would be great because, in general, kids don't want to leave home no matter what."

Jason looked at the floor. He felt so uncomfortable he suddenly changed the subject.

"Guess what we had for supper last night."

"I can't guess . . . ice cream?"

"No. A steak!" he said. "With fries."

"Yummy," she said. But she knew by looking at

Jason's reddening face that he was covering something up. In fact, there had been beans from a can and a package of chips. But it wasn't food that was bothering Jason.

"We always want to make certain young people know, Jason, that they will not be taken out of their homes unless there is a very good reason," Mrs. Housemore said. "A lot of thought and consideration go into any decision that leads to splitting up a family. There are no hurried decisions unless there is an obvious reason to act fast. Only if there is reason to think children are in serious danger are they taken away from home immediately. The courts and schools want children to stay with their families, but they also want them to be safe and cared for.

"Jason," said Mrs. Housemore, "we are not sure that you will ever need to leave home. However, if you think you want to move to your Aunt Grace's, that's something we need to talk more about."

After school that day Jason went straight to Aunt Grace's house. As always she greeted him with open arms. He felt warm inside right away. He looked around the little sitting room into the kitchen behind it. But he didn't know how to bring up what was on his mind.

"You have plenty of space here," he said hesitantly.

"Yes," she said, "it's just right for me. When your uncle was alive, it always felt a little crowded. Of course, he was such a big man he took up more than his share of the place. He had to stoop down to go through the door to the kitchen. He seemed to fill up any room he was in. Just the same, how I wish he were still here."

This was the opening Jason was waiting for. He would take a chance.

"I've been thinking, Aunt Grace, that things are kind of tough at home. You know how Dad is."

"I certainly do!" she said, emphasizing the *do* and rolling her eyes toward the ceiling. Jason was relieved.

"I was thinking . . . maybe you'd like me to help you out . . . like stay here in the spare room and do the heavy stuff like the storm windows and the garden, and wash the windows and go to the store and mop the kitchen floor. I'll even kill cockroaches." He stumbled over his words. He didn't wait for her answer for fear she would say no.

"And then you'd have me here if you needed me and I'd be quiet and anyhow, I'd be at school all day and wouldn't get in your way at all." He talked like a salesman thinking up every point in his favor.

"I hadn't thought about it, Jason. What would your mom and dad say?" she asked.

"I haven't asked them. But they wouldn't care. I'd be right down the street from them. They wouldn't mind. They'd hardly notice."

"That's very unlikely, Jason. Let me think it over. It sounds like it might be a good idea, for both you and me. I'll talk to your mom and dad. It might just work, you know." She looked peaceful as she sat there thinking. In fact, Jason had never seen her so quiet.

"Maybe I should talk to Mom tonight," he said eagerly.

"Okay, Jason, you do the exploring. You never know, maybe you've found one solution to two problems."

KAREN'S STORY

Even when there is fighting and danger, as there was in Jason's home, children still feel loyal to their families. On the other hand, some feel so ashamed they talk only about the good things at home so that no one will suspect what really goes on. They worry that if the authorities find out what is happening, their parents will have to go to jail, or they themselves will be taken away from home. Here is the story of Karen, who kept her secret even after she had been badly abused.

Karen was a sixth grader in a school where Mrs. Housemore used to work. Karen came in one day with bruises around her mouth and on her forehead. Her teacher didn't say anything until the next day, when she noticed more signs of physical abuse. She had burns on the backs of her hands.

"Karen, would you like to go see the nurse?" her teacher asked. "You should have something put on those blisters."

"They're nothing," said Karen, and she put her hands under her desk. But the bruises, which were now turning yellow, were visible danger signs. Her teacher asked her to come see her after class. They both went to the nurse's office. Mrs. Housemore was called in, too. They all sat down together. Karen immediately began to cry.

"I can't help it," she said. "I'm not supposed to tell about my mom and dad, but my friend told me that keeping secrets doesn't work. She's right, I guess. The secret is that I fell down the stairs the other night in my sleep. And this morning I tried to turn on the stove, and I got these burns. Nothing's wrong. I'm fine." And she then cried even harder.

It was clear that Karen was covering up the truth. They all knew Karen's family needed help. They told Karen that most children felt the way she did. They didn't want to talk about what was really happening at home. Karen finally agreed that her mother was sick and was having a hard time managing the household and her four children.

Karen's father had left soon after the baby was

born. Since then her mother had been drinking and taking lots of pills. Karen didn't know what the pills were, but she knew that bottle after bottle had been brought into the house by a friend who worked in a nearby drugstore. Karen also admitted that when her mother was drunk, she would hit the children—all of them. Finally, Karen told about how she had to pick up around the house and buy the food after the baby was born. She had been embarrassed when she went alone to cash her mother's checks at the neighborhood supermarket.

But Karen had been afraid to say anything because she had worried that her mother might be forced to leave and go into the hospital. Or worse, the police might come and take her away. Or maybe they'd take all the kids and place them with strangers. Maybe she would be separated from her sisters and baby brother. Also, she had heard that the twin boys in her class were living with foster parents. She didn't know what that meant, but it sounded terrible. She didn't want anything like that to happen to her or her brother and sisters.

RESPONSIBILITIES

There are many things for which children like Karen or even older children should not have to be responsible. Children should never have to take care of their younger brothers and sisters; they should not have to take care of their parents. One fifteen-year-old boy set rules for his mother. He told her she could have no more than two beers at a time, and he flushed the liquor down the toilet. Acting like a parent to your mother is not right.

Children should not have to take charge of money to be sure it isn't lost. They should not be asked for or made to give money to parents to support drug habits. They should not be forced to beg for money, or steal for their parents. Chil-

dren should not have to run households, do all
the cleaning, dishes, cooking, errands, and laun-
dry. These are the responsibilities of parents.

This does not mean children shouldn't take an
interest in their homes. Depending on their ages,
they can do a lot. For example, they can empty
the garbage, clean their own rooms, set the table,
or take care of pets and plants. But they cannot
be expected to take on the task of managing a
household. If parents can't do it, sometimes families must break up.

RUNNING AWAY

There are times when things become so unbear-
able that children think about running away.

"Why don't you run away if things are so bad at
home?" a boy was advised by a friend. He took
his friend's advice, and one night he packed his
clothing in his book bag and climbed out the
basement window. He had planned on leaving for

good. But when he closed the window behind him and the lock snapped from the inside, he became terrified. The night was cold, and he began to shiver. He immediately tried to think of a way to get back in. He pictured his own warm bed, and he wished he were in it. He ran around to the front door. It was locked, too. Finally he had to ring the doorbell and face his parents.

Some runaways end up being prostitutes on the streets because they need money in order to eat and to pay for a place to stay. They may be harmed for life. They do not enjoy what they have to do; most of the time they are miserable. These children are being sexually abused. What they are doing is against the law, and sooner or later they will be picked up by the police. Then the police are required, by law, to call the parents and tell them where their child is, and a parent must be present when the child is questioned.

If a child is thinking about running away, it's best to ask for help first, and to think twice before doing anything. But if he or she does run away, many towns have runaway shelters. Information about them is available from youth centers, the police department, hospitals, and clinics.

In some areas there are families with whom children can stay for several nights, until things improve in their own homes. The police, family clinics, doctors, social workers, youth counselors, and many others have lists of these homes. In these homes no one will call the child's parents to tell them where their child is without that child's permission. But these homes are only temporary shelters.

Sometimes a youth counselor can help parents and a child work something out so the child will feel all right about going back home. It may just take a phone call. Or it may take a meeting in which the counselor, the parents, and the child work together to solve the problem. Most important, children who want to run away should know there are safe places to go.

Any child who has to leave home is lucky if he

or she has a relative like Jason's Aunt Grace. It's much more difficult to move in with a foster family, particularly if they are strangers. Most children want very much to have their families stay together or near one another. At the same time, all children who live with parents who take drugs or drink too much worry about having to leave home. They worry about going to a strange place, such as a group home, because they really don't know what to expect. When they go, they feel abandoned by their own families, and therefore, they are very frightened.

GROUP HOMES

A group home is usually a part of a larger institution. Generally, it houses fewer than twelve children. Two or three children share a room, and it's set up very much like a family. Some group homes are coed, but most are not. The people who work there and take care of just about everything in the house are called houseparents.

Houseparents help children when they first arrive in a group home. There are a lot of new things to learn, such as which rooms and beds are theirs, where to put their clothing, which bathrooms they are supposed to use, where to keep towels, washcloths, and toothbrushes, what time the family eats, when to leave for school, how to get there, and any special house rules. Sometimes the answers to these questions are written out for them, and then they feel comfortable more quickly. If they are still puzzled, all they have to do is ask their houseparents or their caseworkers.

However, even under the best of circumstances children still miss their own parents, sisters, and brothers. They miss their friends and neighbors. They are often homesick, no matter how rough it has been at home. In most cases, however, they soon find a friend or friends in the house. Then there is someone to talk to, walk to school with, or answer questions.

It happens sometimes that a home away from

home has its problems. Some children complain about the lack of privacy or the food. One boy said his roommate kept him awake at night by talking in his sleep. A girl was scratched on her arms and face by another girl because she would not agree to be her best friend. Houseparents may be stricter than a child's own parents because they are responsible for all the children who live with them. However, houseparents are generally people who like children and try to make them feel like part of the family. Eventually, things work out.

FOSTER HOMES

A foster home is simply a family that shares its home, sometimes for a short period of time and sometimes for good, with a child who has no place to live. When children have to leave home, they may be given some idea of how long it will be before they can be reunited with their families. Sometimes, however, we all have to face the hard facts. Some families do not get together again. Some children must remain in foster families or institutions for good. Some are legally adopted.

Nevertheless, many of the same feelings and fears arise as do for children sent to group homes. Children in foster homes feel betrayed by their own families and are therefore frightened and angry, too. In addition, they don't know what to expect. They must learn the family ways. Foster parents may favor their own children without realizing it. However, some children feel at home right away. Others are relieved to be out of the turmoil of their own households, but most continue to feel homesick, at least for a while.

Some parents who take too many drugs die of drug overdoses, or they go to mental hospitals or are killed in drug-related accidents, or they are arrested and go to prison for long periods of time. These unhappy endings do happen. But children need to go on and make the best of their lives whether it's with relatives, in foster homes or group homes, or with the parents who have adopted them.

5

Drugs Are Not Fun

JASON

Jason unlocked the back door. He knew right away his father wasn't home. There was no smell of smoke; the familiar checked jacket wasn't hanging on the hook inside the door. He was relieved. He wasn't going to have to face his dad, who had been high the night before and who would probably be nasty now.

He slung his book bag down on the kitchen floor and opened the fridge. He poured himself a glass of milk, gulped it down, and slouched into the living room. This would be a good time to turn on the TV. He would forget about his talk with Mrs. Housemore, and he would have a peaceful time until the others came home. As he sat down in his father's worn chair, he noticed the remains of a marijuana roach, snuffed out in a plate on the floor. He had never taken a puff. He had always wondered what it would be like. Now would be the time to try. Just one puff, he said to himself. Surely one puff couldn't hurt.

Jason looked around and found a match. He lit it, picked up the roach, held the match to the end of the paper, and took a hesitant puff. He waited. Ronny was right. Nothing happened.

What's the big deal? he said to himself. Then he tried taking a deeper breath and took another puff, forgetting that he'd promised himself only one. After a little while he felt dizzy. Then he began to cough, but he kept on anyway. Then he got scared.

It was time for his mom to come home from work. Supposing she caught him. He took the rest of the butt, ran to the bathroom, and flushed it. Yuck, he said to himself. He went upstairs and took a shower.

What would he tell Mrs. Housemore? He hoped she would think he was sensible for having stopped when he had. He would tell her that it was no big thing, and that he wouldn't smoke again. The boys in his neighborhood had been trying to get him to "do drugs." He'd been able to say no, even though some of them called him a baby and some wouldn't have anything to do with him.

The next day in Mrs. Housemore's office it was easy to talk.

"Sometimes it seems like magic, Jason, but kids are often likely to develop similar characteristics to their parents, even though they don't realize it. Has anyone ever told you that your smile is just like your mom's? I met her once last year to talk with her about Ronny's absences, and now I see your smile and hers are identical. You may not be conscious of imitating them, but it was by listening to your parents, of course, that you first learned how to speak. It is from your parents that you inherit physical characteristics, too." Mrs. Housemore looked down at Jason's collapsed sneakers. "Whom do your flat feet come from? Your mother? Whether you like them or not, Jason, these physical characteristics and mannerisms will probably be with you for life.

"In your family, Jason, your dad has become dependent on several drugs. We know he smokes a lot of pot and uses cocaine. And I wouldn't be at all surprised if he was getting other drugs as well. And your mom is taking more pills than she should. That all adds up to the fact that you are more likely to have problems with drugs than many of your friends. Scientists now know that drug addiction runs in families, so you in particular need to be very careful if you try any kind of drug. That includes marijuana, coffee, cigarettes, many medications, and alcoholic beverages, such as beer, wine, and liquor. It also includes cocaine, crack, and all the stimulants, sedatives, and hallucinogens.

"Jason, you were lucky, but that isn't the case with everybody," said Mrs. Housemore. "Some young people try a drug, and they soon want to try it again. Then they find they can't stop. In many cases it only takes a few smokes before you feel you absolutely must have more. It gets to be as important as air and water." Then she added in a stern voice, *"Drugs are particularly risky for children who have parents who use them.*

"We know that kids start taking drugs for many different reasons. It was your curiosity that made you take a drag on your father's joint. Other kids say that they take drugs to make them feel happy, to feel nothing or to numb out, to forget, to relax before they go to a party, or to feel grown up. One girl said that she felt 'normal' only when she was drinking. Other children say they feel better about themselves when they're high. But they soon learn that the effects don't last long and the letdown is miserable. Some of them have found that by eleventh or twelfth grade their drug habit has trapped them in a cycle of more and more drug use. They find out that drugs do not solve problems; they just put them off until later. What you do is up to you. My advice is that you never try any drug again."

Even though some of his friends tried to get him drunk the very next Saturday night, Jason was able to fight off the pressure from them. They said he was "retarded" and partying with him was a drag. Weekend after weekend they kept trying to get him to take capsules they called reds. They also bought something to smell and tried to get him to join them in sniffing it. But he didn't give in.

One day after classes Jason was talking to the boy whose locker was next to his. He told Jason that a senior had asked him if he could keep crack and a bag of empty vials in his locker.

"What am I going to do?" he asked Jason. "I don't like the idea. . . . I could get caught with the stuff."

"No way do you let him keep it there," said Jason. "If you get caught, they blame you, not him. You're the one who could get into serious trouble— expelled or suspended for having drugs on school property. Or you're the one who gets arrested for possession . . . or maybe with the intent to sell, if he keeps enough there."

"Yeah, I know. But this big kid said he's going to beat me up if I don't help him out. See, he knows my locker is the last place anyone's going to look for anything. He knows I don't use drugs. And he knows that since I belong to SADD, that's Students Against Driving Drunk, and started the BAD Club, that's Boys Against Drugs, no one's gonna go through my stuff."

"What's the BAD Club?" asked Jason.

"A bunch of guys."

"But what do you do in this lousy town?"

"There's plenty to do. We have our bikes, and we have a clubhouse in that broken-down car in the Bentsens' backyard. We play cards. We talk about cars and girls. Do you know Lila?"

"Yeah, I've seen her."

"She comes around sometimes. We hang out. We do a lot of eating—like peanut butter on frozen bananas. Eli's mom is great. She gives us food handouts—something different every day. Last summer we had cookouts nearly every night."

"So?"

"We're not into drugs. Two other guys and I have dads who are addicts—cocaine. We play ball at the Police Athletic League field. Have you ever played ball with cops? It's not bad. They're around there after school. They also have a basketball court at the 'Y', and a boxing team. We have parties all the time. Last week Gus had a haircut, so we celebrated with a bubble gum contest. I blew the biggest. We celebrate just about anything. Mostly we hang out in safe homes where we know no one's going to bring out the booze or take any drugs."

"Cool," said Jason. But then he had to think about going home.

MORE TIPS FROM MRS. HOUSEMORE

If someone in your family is taking drugs, there are certain signs or tips you should watch for so that you don't fall into the same trap Jason did. Here is the list Mrs. Housemore gave to Jason:

1. You may be urged by a parent to "take a sip" or to "try a puff."

2. You may notice that your parent is sometimes happier after a drug has been taken. You may be tempted to look for the same "high."

3. Drugs, medications, and liquor may be easily available in your home. Your curiosity may get the best of you, so you may try something you've found around the house.

4. You may have gotten the message from a parent that an easy way to solve problems is to take a drink or a pill. Or you may notice that a party without some kind of drug isn't considered much fun.

If you *ever* feel you have a drug problem, or find yourself drinking too much, give yourself this test:

1. Do you turn down drugs if they are offered to you?

2. Do your friends or family say anything to you about your use of drugs? Do you lie to them about your drinking or use of drugs?

3. Have you thought about the effect drugs have on you?

4. Do you count on friends to drink or use drugs with you?

5. Do you use drugs before, during, or after school?

6. Do you hide drugs at home or in your school locker?

7. Do you drink or get high before you meet friends or go to a party?

8. When you go to a party, are drugs nearly always part of the "scene"?

9. Do you get high or drunk every day? Every week? Every month?

If you answer "yes" or "often" to *one* of these questions, you have a problem. If you ever need help, remember that children are never punished when they ask qualified people for help. On the contrary, if they need help, they're told how to get it.

6

Treatment
and Recovery

JASON

Jason still worried a lot. He began to fear that
his father might die. His father had horrible
shakes every morning. He couldn't hold his cup
steadily enough to get it up to his lips without
spilling the coffee. Even though he was very thin,

he never ate with the family. He stayed in bed nearly all day. When he got up, it was to make a quick trip to the liquor store or to "cop some dope" from his dealer.

Jason knew where they met. He had told Mrs. Housemore about the meetings with the dealer. He had followed his father one evening, hiding a few feet behind him in the bushes. He had seen him hand some cash to a young boy who seemed about Jason's age. The boy gave Jason's father a small bag. They nodded to each other. Then the boy walked off quickly, and Jason's father stumbled back toward the house. As he climbed up the front steps, Jason let himself in the back door. His father never knew he'd been followed. He didn't even know that Jason had been out of the house.

In the house, as soon as he saw his father, Jason knew he'd had too much of something.

"This house is a pigpen. You're a slob. You don't care, do you?" his father yelled at his mother. Then he started an argument with Ronny.

"Why do you always slam the door? Go sweep the basement steps and get out of the way."

The next day at Mrs. Housemore's Jason came right out with it.

"Things are getting worse," he said. "My dad sleeps all day. When Mom comes home, they fight. He yells at us, too. He threatens to punch us, but he's only hit us a few times. We know when to move. But Mom just stands there and takes it. Then he goes out, gets more booze or maybe even cocaine, comes home, lights a joint, and goes back to bed. I wish he'd get out. Sometimes I think about turning him in. But I know I can't squeal on my own father. Maybe it's time for me to move to my Aunt Grace's," Jason said.

Mrs. Housemore smiled. "That sounds like a good idea for now."

Jason squeezed his stuff into an old knapsack he kept under his bed. He packed his comb, his denim jacket, his Mets cap, his favorite T-shirts, and the latest issue of *Sports Illustrated*. Then, just to keep his mother from complaining, he snatched his vitamins off the kitchen table. He had made all the necessary plans with his Aunt Grace. She had wanted Jason to move in the very day he made the suggestion, but he hadn't been quite ready.

Now he talked to his mother about the move.

"You can go if you really want to," she said, "as long as Ronny stays to help. I'll miss you, though.

You're my baby, you know. But you won't be that far away, right? I want you to come by for clean clothes every other day. You'll come by?"

"Sure, Ma," Jason said.

"But you better speak to your father." Tears came to her eyes.

Jason carefully planned to talk to his father early the next morning, before he'd had anything to smoke or drink. He's pretty together this morning, thought Jason. This will be the best time.

"Dad, I'm going to stay with Aunt Grace for a while. She needs me around the house, and she's agreed to let me have her spare room. I'm moving over this afternoon."

"Go!" said Jason's dad, waving his hand as if he were brushing off a fly.

The hassle Jason expected didn't happen. His father just didn't care. Or at least he didn't seem to care. Luckily his talks with Mrs. Housemore had prepared him for this blow.

This man is sick, he said to himself. He can't care for anyone. It's not just me. Jason tried hard not to feel totally rejected. But soon after the talk his head began to ache.

While Jason stayed at Aunt Grace's, Ronny kept

him up to date on what was happening at home.

"Dad won't leave the house, and the fights with Mom are fierce," Ronny reported when they met on the way to school. "Last night she spent the evening in the basement just to get out of his way. You've got it made, Jason. I wish I were over at Aunt Grace's, too."

"So, why don't you just come? I have a double bed. No one would care."

"Nah," said Ronny. "Mom's really into the pills. I gotta be home if you're not there, stupid."

"So, make me feel lousy," Jason said. But he wondered about his mother and the Valium.

Several nights later there was a phone call. As soon as he heard Ronny's voice, he knew something was wrong.

"Well, it's happened! You missed it all. Dad came at her with that big knife. What a scene! It was some struggle to keep out of his way. I watched Mom. She pointed to the phone. I dialed nine-one-one . . . nearly got the cops on the phone. Was I ever scared. But before they answered, Dad dropped the knife, and then, guess what, he got down on the floor . . . I couldn't believe it . . . and he was crying, right out loud. And he said that he didn't know what he was doing, he thought he was going crazy and he needed help!"

"Really? Then what?"

"What do you think, you wimp? Mom and I kind of pulled him along the floor. It was no fun getting him into the car. We drove to the hospital, and we got back real late. She didn't say much today, but I guess he's in bad shape."

"Come on, Ronny, what else?"

"I don't know, but I think things might get better."

That was the beginning of a long road to health for Jason's father, and a new life for the whole family. Jason's father went straight from the hospital to a recovery center. The others traveled there weekly for family therapy. Much to Jason's surprise, his mother's pill taking was brought up by Ronny in the very first family session. He then realized why Ronny had been so firm about not moving out. Ronny had always been the "caretaker," the counselor said. The counselor also labeled Jason as the "quiet one" because he escaped from the family conflict by going up to his room, down to the basement, or out of the house.

After that, their mother admitted she was taking more and more pills and couldn't stop. The family therapist gave her the name of another counselor, so she could have help for herself.

Jason's father was away from home for nearly three months. While he was away, Jason moved back home, though he wished he could have stayed with Aunt Grace. This was the kind of home he wanted. There was no crying, no doors banging in the middle of the night, and no one shoved him around or put him down for just being himself.

When Jason's father finally came home, he seemed like a stranger. He was quiet and serious. Every day he dressed carefully and went to look for work. In the evenings he left the house regularly to go to meetings. Now he was practically never home, and that was a relief to Jason. When he was home, he was usually talking on the phone to his Narcotics Anonymous or Alcoholics Anonymous friends. Anyhow, Jason didn't know what to talk to him about. Should he ask him about what happened at the recovery facility? What the other people were like? What they did all day?

He and his dad used to spend hours in the yard with the car—tinkering with the engine and

polishing the exterior. Would his father still be
interested? Would his father want to know about
his grades? Or how many homers he had hit? Or
what he and his friends were doing? He'd have to
wait and see. He didn't want to say the wrong thing.

The whole family was different; his father wasn't
the only one. Jason's mom talked a lot about how
they should all "take life one day at a time" and
should "trust in a higher power." Jason had seen
these slogans on the wall at the recovery center.
But his mother was the last to change. Finally she
threw the Valium in the garbage. After that she
insisted they all go together to meetings. She took
the alcoholic drinks, including the beer, out of the
house. She also canceled party invitations with
friends.

As time went on, the family began to talk to each
other more. On Sundays they ate breakfast together.
They had cookouts, they went to the movies, and
that spring, for the first time ever, Jason's father
asked them if they'd like to drive up into the
mountains to camp out for a few days. Jason
thought he was living in a dream. He prayed that it
wouldn't come to an end. But if it did, he knew he
could go back to Aunt Grace's.

Just before the end of school that year Jason

dropped by to see Mrs. Housemore. He stuck his head in through her office door.

"Guess what," he said. "I got an A in math."

TREATMENT

A sick person should have the chance to get the care he or she needs. No one should have to wait until he is forced to leave home because he is caught using illegal substances and arrested. There are many people who choose to go into treatment before their illness leads them into deep trouble with the law. People who are addicted and sick need health care. That care should come from doctors who specialize in treating addictions and recovering addicts, or from health professionals, such as counselors, social workers, or psychologists.

People don't become addicted on purpose. When they start using drugs, it probably never occurs to them how much harm drug use could do to their families and to themselves. However, they need to stop denying that they are sick, and they must want to make a change. Then they will be able to take the first step toward asking for the help they need.

OUTPATIENT CARE

Some people are able to stop using drugs and alcohol by going to Alcoholics Anonymous (AA), Cocaine Anonymous (CA), or Narcotics Anonymous (NA) meetings. There they make a firm commitment to stop drinking and to stop using drugs at least for one day at a time. Other addicts don't choose any of these, but get help from therapists who may meet with them individually or in groups with others suffering an addiction.

INPATIENT CARE

Those who are very sick or can't stop taking drugs on their own may need to go to a hospital or recovery facility. These vary a great deal, but in general, patients remain there for at least a month.

The early part of recovery is what doctors call detoxification. During this phase the addict must stay off drugs so that the body becomes accustomed to living without them. As people are withdrawn from drugs, they have physiological symptoms, such as sweats, shakes, and nausea. In general, this process takes only a few days, and then the addicted person begins to feel better. How sick a person will feel as the drugs leave the body will depend on which drugs he has been taking, how much of the drugs he used, and how they affected his health.

After detoxification the real work begins. The more the family understands, the easier it will be for both the addict and for them. When all the drugs are out of his system, the addicted person will have to learn to live a different kind of life. That means finding work if he has lost a job, and getting on better terms again with the family. He will have to make new friends, too. They will probably be the people from AA or NA meetings. The addict will also have to learn what to do during the times when he used to be high, drunk, or spaced out. This takes courage, work, time . . . and a family that understands.

FAMILY INVOLVEMENT

It is often a relief for the family to have the addicted person out of the house for a while, particularly if he or she is in treatment. And it may be easier for the addict to be away from the stress and temptations at home in order to concentrate on getting well. When people go into treatment, they are making an honest effort to recover.

Children often think that if a parent is sick, it is up to that person to get off the drug or drugs. As Jason found out, treatment is not just for the alcoholic or drug addict. The whole family has to take part in it. Addicts need all the help they can get. Therefore, even if you think the addiction problem is your parent's, you will probably be asked to go to meetings at the recovery center or hospital and learn more about your family and how you can get along together.

HELP FOR CHILDREN

There should also be special help for you. A counselor may suggest that you go to a self-help group, such as Alateen, Al-Anon, or Nar-Anon. These are known as "twelve-step programs" because they use the same steps to recovery that are the basis of Alcoholics Anonymous. In meetings you will learn how to rely on a "higher power" for help in living with a parent who takes drugs. The meetings are held every week in the same place, and they are free. Most school guidance counselors have lists of times and places of meetings. In addition, Alcoholics Anonymous or Al-Anon

Family Groups are listed in the phone book. You can find out where and when the meetings are held by calling these groups.

You may have to ask for a ride or some kind of help to get to meetings. It is possible that your parents won't permit you to go to meetings, particularly if they are worried or ashamed of what the family is going through. They also might refuse to let you go if the meetings are held at night. Find out if there are daytime meetings in or near your school. Then your chances of going will be better.

Whether or not your parent is in treatment, you will probably get a lot out of any meetings you attend. You don't have to be shy because you'll find when you get there that there will be other children who have problems very much like yours. In fact, you may be very surprised at some of the things you hear because you may never have imagined that personal feelings could be shared or talked about in public. However, no one will insist that you talk if you don't want to say anything. You can just listen. Eventually, you will feel less nervous and more sure of yourself. You will no longer feel so alone.

If you can't get to an Alateen or Al-Anon meeting, there are other kinds of help for you in addition to student assistance counseling. Many schools have drug guidance counselors, teen leaders, or peer support groups. Most school guidance people will be helpful in finding what is right for you.

NEVER GIVE UP

You should keep in mind that people who have been addicted to drugs can stop getting worse and start getting better. But they are never cured. There is always a chance that they may use drugs or drink again.

If your parent does go for help and does get better, you should know ahead of time that one part of getting well may include a slip backward. Even when a family is prepared, this is always discouraging. If your parent gets treatment, you can hope that won't happen. Some recovering addicts are able to stay sober or drug-free after their first try. But for some there may be more than one slip.

Don't forget, there is always hope for recovery. It may take time, but families should never give up. As you continue to hope and want the best for your family, you need to lead your own life to its fullest, no matter what happens.

7

Summary:
The Facts About Drugs

WHAT IS A DRUG?

A drug is any substance that affects how people feel, think, and act. However, it is important to understand that drugs affect different people in different ways. The way a drug affects any one person depends on the kind of drug taken, how much of it is taken, how often it is used, how quickly it gets to the brain, and what other drugs are being used at the same time. There are some people who are more sensitive to drugs than others, so that even a small dose will have a strong effect. In fact, it is just about impossible to predict how anyone will react to a specific drug. This unpredictability is one reason drugs are so dangerous. You never know what can happen.

College students sometimes take dares during beer parties, and often one of them will get sick. An overdose can cause death if too much is taken too quickly. Remember, this can happen to anyone who takes a drug.

DRUG CLASSIFICATIONS

Drugs are classified according to their effects:

1. **Stimulants** are known as uppers. They make people feel "high" or peppy. Coffee is a mild stimulant. Amphetamines or pep pills are stronger stimulants. Cocaine (or

crack) is one of the strongest and most dangerous stimulants. When the effects of a stimulant wear off, people feel tired and down in the dumps or sick. They may be unable to take care of their daily responsibilities. If the effects are bad enough, the user might become mentally or physically disabled, or both.

2. **Depressants or sedatives** are known as downers or escape drugs. They relax muscles and make people feel drowsy and confused. Users say depressants make them feel spaced out or sleepy. These drugs include barbiturates, Librium, Valium, and alcohol. Alcohol is always found in liquid form. The other depressants are found in pill form or liquids that are injected into veins. Most sedatives must be prescribed by a physician. On the other hand, alcohol is easily obtained. A person who has taken a

sedative or depressant drug certainly should not try to ride a bicycle, dance, take part in sports, or do anything that requires physical coordination.

3. **Hallucinogens** are also known as mind changers. They distort what is seen, heard, or felt. They change reality, so that a ticking watch might sound like a hammer pounding, or a red stoplight could look as bright as the sun. One teenager reported that after she took LSD, a strong hallucinogen, she saw snakes and heard them hissing. Actually she was hearing steam leaking from a nearby radiator. PCP is an hallucinogen that kills pain. It also distorts reality and causes confusion.

4. **Narcotics** are pain-killers. Most of them contain or resemble opium. They include codeine, methadone, Demerol™,

morphine, and heroin. When people abuse these drugs, they can feel anxious, depressed, and sleepy.

Heroin is the most commonly abused narcotic. It is usually injected into the veins. If unclean needles are used, infections, such as AIDS (acquired immune deficiency syndrome), can be spread. Heroin is also especially dangerous because it is extremely addictive.

DRUG EFFECTS

Physical Addiction

When a drug is used over and over again, the body becomes adjusted to it, and the person needs more and more to get the same effect. This is called tolerance. When the drug taking is stopped, the body, which has become accustomed to having it, will continue to feel as if the drug is still needed. The person will then feel extremely uncomfortable. He or she may shake, sweat, and feel nauseated and will feel normal again only if he or she goes back to taking the drug. A person is physically addicted to a drug when he or she has developed tolerance and suffers when the drug is stopped.

Psychological Addiction

Sometimes people feel or think they can't do without a certain drug even though their bodies don't crave it and they have no physical symptoms when they stop using it. This feeling is known as psychological dependence. It occurs when an individual continues to use a drug that gives a feeling of well-being.

LEGAL DRUGS

Caffeine is a legal drug found in coffee, tea, and soft drinks. Surprisingly, chocolate also contains caffeine. Legal drugs also include nicotine, which is found in tobacco. However, young people under a certain age cannot legally buy tobacco products, such as cigarettes, cigars, and chewing tobacco. Alcohol, too, is a special case. Only adults over a certain age may drink, serve, or sell it. For underage persons, it is an illegal drug.

There are hundreds of drugs sold legally over the counter in supermarkets, general stores, and drugstores. You've probably seen them lined up on shelves or advertised on TV. They include pain-killers, cough medicines, diet pills, and many more. Anyone can buy them, but that doesn't mean they are safe. Labels on containers should be read carefully before these easily obtainable drugs are used.

Prescription Drugs

Prescription drugs are those ordered by a physician or dentist who is licensed by the state. These drugs are considered medicines and should be taken in the exact amounts and frequency suggested by a doctor. Remember that drugs can have unexpected side effects. For example, diet pills may take away a big appetite, but they can also make the heart beat faster than it should.

Some people become addicted to prescription drugs, most often a pill of some sort that was first given to help. One woman became addicted to the Valium given to her by a doctor for a painful backache caused by tension. The Valium helped her feel better at the time. However, it didn't help in the long run because of its side effects. It made her groggy, and she once fell asleep while driving.

ILLEGAL DRUGS

Illegal drugs are prohibited by the United States Food and Drug Administration from being sold or used unless they are prescribed. Drugs are not to be fooled with. If used carelessly, any drug can do permanent damage. Sometimes people think they are using a drug carefully, but they can be poisoned because a harmful substance or an ingredient unknown to the user has been added. Illegal drugs are prepared with little regard for human safety, and there are no guarantees of purity.

No one ever plans to become addicted, but addiction can sneak up on anyone. It may take only a matter of days to become addicted to crack. Addiction to alcohol often takes years. Once you've started taking such drugs as cocaine, nicotine, heroin, and alcohol, it becomes terribly difficult to stop. You may have seen your mother or father try to stop smoking. It is not easy. Although it is not the case for cigarette smokers, some people on other drugs must be hospitalized in order to get over their drug habits. In the hospital the person not only is removed from access to the drug itself, but is helped to recover physically from the drug's effects and to find ways to live without it.

Now that you know what drugs are, you can

watch out for them, and you can make sure that you won't slip into a drug habit because you don't know what you are doing. You can be alert to the dangers of all drugs and decide now that, even though you have a parent who takes them, drugs are not for you.